Reading Brainstorms

by
Becky Daniel

illustrated by Nancee McClure

Cover by Nancee McClure

Copyright © Good Apple, Inc., 1990

Good Apple, Inc.
1204 Buchanan St., Box 299
Carthage, IL 62321-0299

All rights reserved. Printed in the United States of America.

Copyright © Good Apple, Inc., 1990

ISBN No. 0-86653-560-8

Printing No. 987654

Good Apple, Inc.
1204 Buchanan St., Box 299
Carthage, IL 62321-0299

The purchase of this book entitles the buyer to reproduce the student activity pages for classroom use only. Any other use requires written permission from Good Apple, Inc.

All rights reserved. Printed in the United States of America.

Table of Contents

Wacky Words	1
Picture That!	2
The Birthday Party	3
Happyville Citizens	4
What's Wrong Here?	5
Reading Pictures	6
It's No Picnic	7
Circus Fun	8
Draw Your Own Story	9
You Must Decide	10
Out the Window!	11
Following Directions	12
Simon Sez	13
Coloring the Animals	14
Happyville Houses	15
Coloring Clowns	16
Changing Letters	17
Hidden Words	18
Conundrums	19
Reading a Graph	20
Check, Please!	21
Riddle Names	22
Scrambled Word Riddles	23
True or False?	24
Recipes for What?	25
What's Inside?	26
Draw It!	27
What Day Is It?	28
Merryville Calendar	29
Read and Think	30
Lamb's Birthday Party	31
Is, Is Not, Is, Is Not!	32
Four Facts	33
Multiple Meanings	34
Colorful Details	35
Happily Ever After?	36
Walking Downtown	37
Which Way?	38
Rhyme Time	39
Alike and Different	40
Word Meaning Zoo	41
Double Meaning Riddles	42
Word Associations	43
You Pick a Pair	44
Funny Relations	45
Reading Pictures	46
A Big Surprise	47
Homonym Zoo	48
Lamb's Little House	49
Eight-Letter Words	50
Hinky Pinkies	51
Making Judgements	52
Generalizations	53
Reading Up and Down	54
Reading Matchup	55
True or False?	56
Crossword Puzzle	57
Rhyming Animals	58
Scrambled Anagrams	59
Anagrams	60
Five Fantastic Gifts!	61
Hidden Colors	62
Who Brought What?	63
Relationships	64
Favorite Colors	65
Occupations	66
What Day of the Week	67
Bez, Poks and Deeks	68
Snack Time	69
Going to School	70
The Great Race!	71
Answer Key	72
Award Certificates	75

To the Teacher

Reading Brainstorms is designed to teach early grade students comprehensive thinking skills. Unfortunately, most elementary reading lessons involve a great deal of rote learning, and one problem facing educators is how to teach our children to think analytically. Children can often read words that they do not comprehend, and although memorization is an important skill, thinking skills are important, too.

To prepare your students to use the work sheets found herein, it is important to realize that reading the directions may be difficult or impossible for beginning readers. It is therefore suggested that the directions be given in small groups and the examples carefully explained before children are sent back to their desks to do independent seatwork.

Reading Brainstorms includes activities to teach comprehension from picture clues, key words, details and main ideas from pictures. Other important thinking skills such as drawing inferences and conclusions, interpreting new ideas and verifying opinions are also covered. The fun-filled puzzles, riddles and activity sheets will make reading comprehension an enjoyable learning experience for all.

Bonus activities are found on many pages. These activities are usually more difficult and should not be a requirement. Use the bonus activities for extra credit. Students that complete these should receive special recognition. A class competition could involve keeping track of how many bonus activities are completed by each student and rewarding those that complete a given number. Awards are found on pages 75 and 76 and a special award certificate for bonus activities is included.

Wacky Words

Can you read these words or phrases by the way they are written? For example, the first one is *highlight*. Write your answers on the line in each box.

1. *light* Answer: _____	5. SHE IS / JOYED Answer: _____
2. *ladiesgentlemen* Answer: _____	6. EGGS / EASY Answer: _____
3. What ⇑ ⇓ Must Answer: _____	7. I'M JUST MYSELF (vertical) Answer: _____
4. league Answer: _____	8. EVERYTHING / Pizza Answer: _____

Bonus: Make up a wacky word of your own. Share it with a friend.

Name _____

Picture That!

Look at the picture carefully as you answer each question found below.

1. Which children have three or more buttons?
2. Which child has the longest hair?
3. Which two children are wearing hats?
4. Which children are playing with a ball?
5. Which child is jumping rope?
6. Which child doesn't have pockets?
7. Which child is wearing sneakers?
8. Which child is not wearing shoes?

Name _____

Copyright © 1990, Good Apple, Inc.

The Birthday Party

Look at the picture carefully as you answer each question found below. Read and think about each question; some may be tricky.

1. How old is the birthday child?
2. How many children did the boy invite to his party?
3. How many of the invited guests are wearing party hats?
4. How many of the invited guests are eating cake but not eating ice cream?
5. How many of the children are eating ice cream but not eating cake?
6. How many boys did the birthday child invite? How many girls?

Bonus: How many animals can you find hidden in the picture?

Name _____

Happyville Citizens

Follow the directions carefully to complete this picture of Happyville.

1. Color Lamb's bow PINK. Color her dress ORANGE. Don't color her wool.
2. Color Rabbit's shorts BLUE. Color the rest of Rabbit BROWN.
3. Color Bear's pants GREEN. Color his pail GREEN. Color the rest of him BLACK.
4. Color Duck's vest your favorite color. Color his bill and feet ORANGE. Color his feathers YELLOW.
5. Finish coloring the picture any colors you choose.

Bonus: Write the directions for coloring the American flag.

Name _____

What's Wrong Here?

At first glance you may think that this is an ordinary classroom, but if you look carefully you will discover twelve things that are wrong. List each one on a line found below the picture.

1. _____
2. _____
3. _____
4. _____
5. _____
6. _____
7. _____
8. _____
9. _____
10. _____
11. _____
12. _____

Name _____

Reading Pictures

If you read the story and study the picture, you will discover that the story and picture tell different tales. Underline the words in the story that do not agree with the picture.

One summer night, three girls were roller skating to the park. Suddenly one girl noticed that her cat was following her. When she saw the cat, she began to cry. She thought that a cat in the park was a very sad thing to see.

Bonus: Can you find two more things that are different in the story and picture?

Name _____

It's No Picnic

Duck is going on a picnic. Lamb is going to school. Read the words found below and decide who will need each item. List the words or draw pictures of the things that Duck will need in Duck's picnic basket. List the words or draw pictures of the things that Lamb will need in Lamb's backpack.

sandwich	**cupcakes**
watermelon	**apple**
crayons	**chips**
napkin	**lunch money**
pickles	**fork**
pencil	**paper plate**
math book	**soda**
homework	**something to share**

Name _____

Circus Fun

Use the picture found below to answer each question.

1. How many animals are in the picture? _____
2. How many animals are wearing hats? _____
3. How many elephants do you see? _____
4. How many legs in the picture? (Count the legs you cannot see. For example, even if you can see only two of an elephant's legs, you know it has four altogether.) _____
5. How many animals are not wearing hats? _____
6. Color the picture any colors you choose.

Name _____

Name _____

Draw Your Own Story

Draw a picture to complete the sentence found in each box below.

1. We went to the zoo and I saw a

2. On my grandfather's farm are many

3. My brother went to the beach and brought home

4. Grandmother gave me a

5. My dad surprised Mom with a new

6. The worm was sitting on a

Name _____

You Must Decide

Look at the picture below and give the appropriate number or numbers to answer each question.

1. Which children are being the quietest? _____
2. Which child could use a dictionary? _____
3. Which child could use a *TV Guide*? _____
4. Which child could use a bookmark? _____
5. Which children may be doing their homework? _____
6. Which child would most likely feel warm and tired? _____

Bonus: Which child is doing the thing you spend the most time doing? Explain.

Out the Window!

Using the four pictures found below, decide which picture represents the correct season when answering each question. Example: Christmas is in the winter, so picture number two would be the best answer for the first question.

1.

2.

3.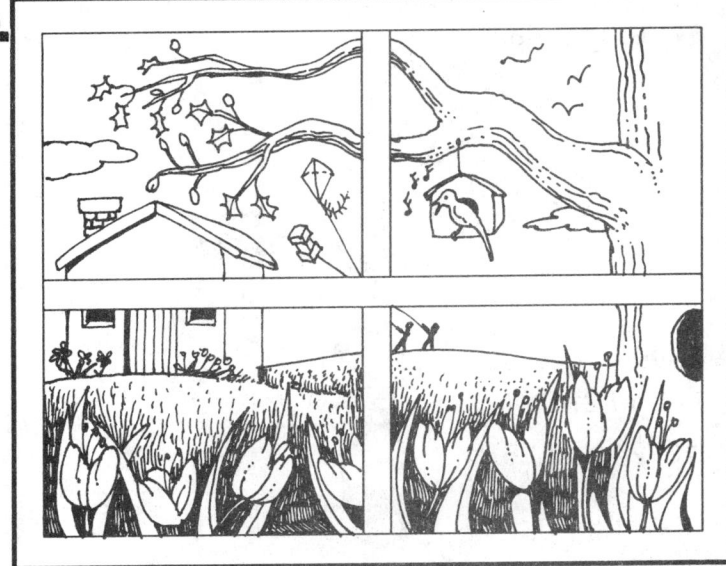

4.

1. Christmas? _____
2. The first day of school? _____
3. The last day of school? _____
4. Halloween? _____
5. The Fourth of July? _____
6. Easter? _____
7. Thanksgiving? _____
8. Your birthday? _____

Bonus: List a holiday for each season of the year.

Name _____

Following Directions

To discover the secret message, follow the directions carefully.

Secret Message:

__ __ __ __ __ __ __ __ __ __ __ __ __ __
1   2   3   4   5   6   7   8   9 10 11 12 13 14

__ __ __ __ __ __ __ __ __ __ __ __ __ __ __
15 16 17 18 19 20 21 22 23 24 25 26 27 28 29

__ __ __ __   __ __ __ __ __ __ __
30 31 32 33   34 35 36 37 38 39 40

1. Put the vowel *A* in spaces 1, 10, 16 and 20.
2. Put the letter *C* in space 6.
3. Put the letter *D* in space 5.
4. Put the vowel *E* in spaces 18, 28, 31, 32 and 39.
5. Put the letter *G* in space 2.
6. Put the letter *H* in space 35.
7. Put the vowel *I* in space 12.
8. Put the letter *J* in space 23.
9. Put the letter *K* in space 17.
10. Put the letter *M* in spaces 8, 15 and 33.
11. Put the letter *N* in spaces 11, 14, 21 and 27.
12. Put the vowel *O* in spaces 3, 4, 7, 13, 24 and 36.
14. Put the letter *P* in space 9.
15. Put the letter *R* in spaces 26, 37 and 40.
17. Put the letter *S* in spaces 19, 30 and 34.
18. Put the letter *T* in space 38.
19. Put the vowel *U* in space 25.
20. Put the letter *Y* in spaces 22 and 29.

Name _____

Simon Sez

To complete this picture, you must read and follow the directions found below.

1. **Give the tall girl RED curly hair.**
2. **Give the small girl blond straight hair.**
3. **Color the tall child's dress ORANGE.**
4. **Color the other girl's dress RED.**
5. **Fill the small girl's basket with PURPLE flowers.**
6. **Draw the sun in the upper right-hand corner of the picture.**
7. **Color the grass GREEN.**
8. **Give the taller child BLUE socks.**
9. **Finish coloring the picture any colors you choose.**

Name _____

Coloring the Animals

Follow the directions carefully as you color the picture found below.

1. Color the animal that flies around at night **BROWN**.
2. Color the animal that would frighten the mouse **ORANGE** with **WHITE** stripes.
3. Color the animal that likes to eat carrots **WHITE** with **BLACK** spots.
4. Color the smallest animal **RED** with **BLACK** spots.
5. Color the animal that barks **WHITE** with **BLACK** spots.
6. Color the animal that stores nuts for the winter **GRAY**.
7. Color the animal that most likely enjoys eating cheese **BLACK**.
8. Color the rest of the picture any colors you choose.

Name _____

Happyville Houses

Follow the directions to complete each house.

1. **Color Rabbit's roof RED.**
2. **Color the roof of the house in the middle ORANGE.**
3. **Draw and color a PURPLE door on Lamb's house.**
4. **Draw and color a BLUE door on Duck's house.**
5. **Draw and color YELLOW bushes on both sides of Lamb's house.**
6. **Draw and color a big GREEN tree between Duck's and Rabbit's houses.**
7. **Draw and color a PINK door on Rabbit's house.**
8. **Duck has mail going out; put the RED flag up on his mailbox.**
9. **Color the roof of Lamb's house GREEN and the rest of her house RED.**
10. **Color the rest of Rabbit's house YELLOW.**
11. **Color the rest of Duck's house PURPLE.**
12. **It is a dark, cloudy day in Happyville. Draw the GRAY clouds and put rain in the sky.**

Name _____

Coloring Clowns

Follow the directions carefully when coloring the four clowns found below.

1. Color the shirt of the clown with a flower on his hat your very favorite color.
2. Color the shirt of the clown with a polka-dot tie the same color as the cover on your bed. If your bed cover has many colors, choose your favorite.
3. Color the pants of the clown with the biggest feet the color of your hair.
4. Color the pants of the clown with three pockets the color of your eyes.
5. Color the shirt of the clown with a striped tie the color of the outside of your house.
6. Color the shirt of the clown juggling balls your favorite color for cars.
7. Color the pants of the clown wearing a sad face the color of your shoes.
8. Color the pants of the clown not wearing a hat the color of the shirt, dress or blouse you are wearing today. If what you are wearing has many different colors, choose your favorite.
9. Finish coloring the picture any colors you choose.

Name _____

Changing Letters

To discover the secret message, follow the directions carefully.

1. Change the letter *X* to *A*.
2. Change the letter *Z* to *E*.
3. Change the letter *C* to *O*.
4. Change the letter *G* to *N*.
5. Change the letter *J* to *T*.
6. Change the letter *K* to *L*.
7. Change the letter *M* to *R*.
8. Change the letter *P* to *S*.
9. Change the letter *Q* to *B*.
10. Change the letter *V* to *I*.
11. Don't change any of the remaining letters.

Secret Message:

q z   x   f m v z g d   j c   y c u m p z k f
___   ___   _____   ___   _____

x g d   c j h z m p   w v k k   x k p c
_____   _____   _____   _____

w x g j j c.
_____

Name _____

17

Copyright © 1990, Good Apple, Inc.   GA1171

Name _____

Hidden Words

Many small words can be found within larger words. Example: Within this girl's name is hidden a boy: Mabel/Abel. Use the riddles found below to list the big words with smaller words found within.

1. **Within this terrible dream there lives a horse.**
   _____

2. **Within this body part there is yet another body part.**
   _____

3. **Within this insect there is another insect.**
   _____

4. **Within this jar of jelly is hidden a body part.**
   _____

5. **Within this insect is hidden a boy.**
   _____

6. **Inside this animal there is a color.**
   _____

Bonus: Within this very special person a cat's lunch is hidden.

Conundrums

A conundrum is a riddle which depends on a pun (double meaning) or homonym (words that sound the same but are spelled differently and have different meanings) in the answer. See how many of these animal conundrums you can guess.

1. What is a barber's favorite animal?
   _____

2. What animal sometimes hits her babies?
   _____

3. What is the most grouchy animal?
   _____

4. What animal is the best dodgeball player?
   _____

5. What animal can stand just about anything?
   _____

6. What animal can dig the deepest holes?
   _____

7. What animal do most people have in their family?
   _____

8. What animal is found at all baseball games?
   _____

Name _____

Bonus: What animal never grows old?

Copyright © 1990, Good Apple, Inc.   19   GA1171

Name _____

Reading a Graph

Use the cookie graph to answer the questions found below.

1. How many children were surveyed? _____
2. Which cookie did half of the children like best? _____
3. How many children like a cookie not listed on the graph? _____
4. Which cookie did five children choose as their favorite? _____
5. How many children picked sugar cookies as their favorite? _____
6. Which of the cookies do you like best? _____

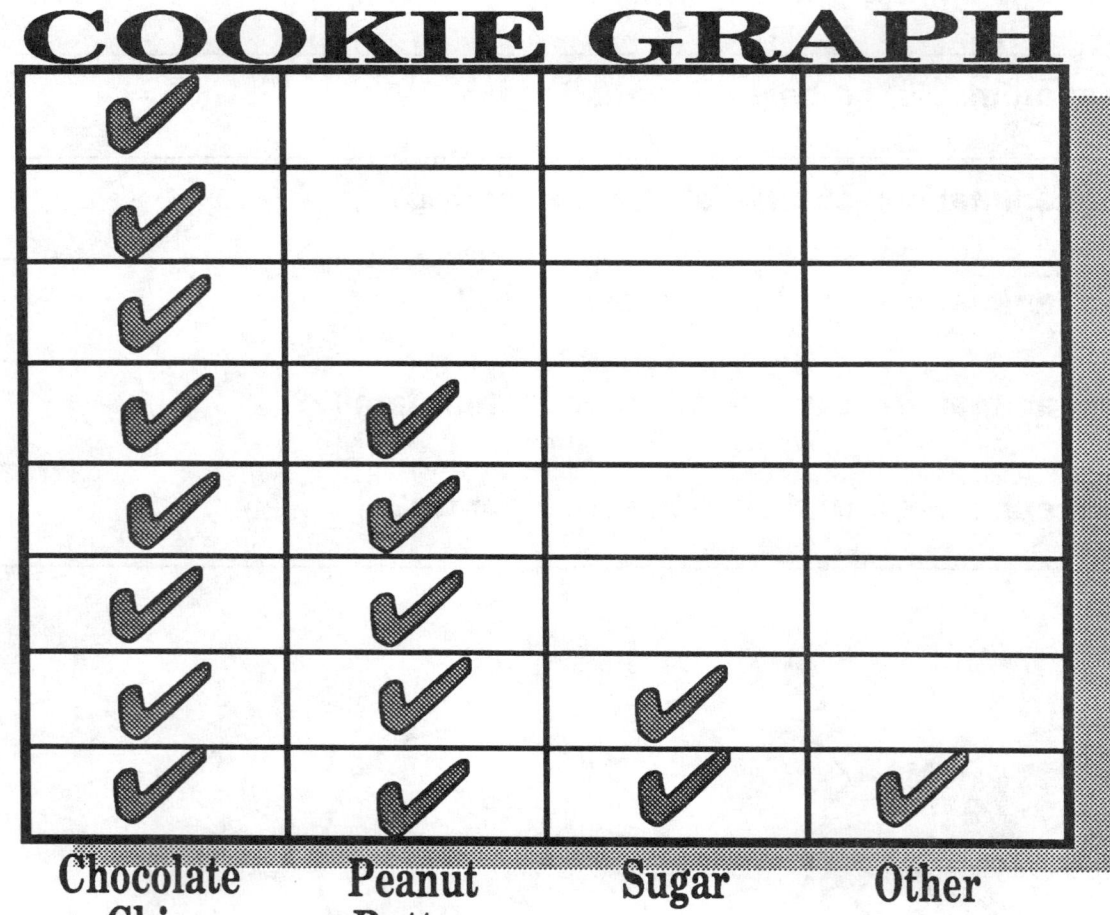

Bonus: Survey sixteen children and create your own cookie graph.

Check, Please!

Put checks in the appropriate places on the chart. For example: A frog can make a noise, so put a check in the last box in the first row.

	can read	talks	needs water	jumps	makes noise
frog					
boys					
plants					
girls					
flower					
fish					
tiger					
stick					
leaf					
computer					

Name _____

Bonus: Can you think of a two-letter word that describes something that needs a check for all of the things listed on the chart?

Riddle Names

When Mr. Furter was a little boy he loved hot dogs so much his mother changed his first name to Frank (frankfurter). Just for fun see how many of the first names you can guess for the riddles found below.

1. Mr. Fold liked money so much they nicknamed him _____.
   His full name is _____.

2. Mr. Id is so shy that his wife calls him _____. His full name is
   _____.

3. Mrs. Tom likes to play the drums so much she named her firstborn son
   _____. His full name is _____.

4. Mr. Kate, the teacher, has a middle initial of *U*. Can you guess his first name? _____ His full name is _____.

5. Mr. Walk is always in such a hurry that when he crosses the street he often gets a ticket for crossing in the wrong place. Can you guess what his first name is? _____ His full name is _____.

Name _____

Bonus: Mr. Torian is fussy and stuffy. Guess what his first name is. _____
His full name is _____.

Name _____

Scrambled Word Riddles

If you correctly combine or unscramble the letters of two words found in each riddle, you will know the answer for each riddle. Example: This tropical fruit will go with any other food that man may serve. (MANGO) Underline the appropriate letters and write the answer for each riddle.

1. This fruit, not at all like an apple, looks a bit like a cone from a pine tree.
   _____

2. This fast food favorite isn't made with ham patties; it is made with beef burger.
   _____

3. You should wear this item of clothing if you are cold and have wet ears.
   _____

4. This baby animal should be sold in a kit with ten per package.
   _____

Bonus: This animal has a thicker peel than most.

True or False?

Read each two-part sentence and decide if both parts of the sentence are true (TT), both parts are false (FF), the first part is true and the second part is false (TF), or the first part is false and the second part is true (FT). Mark each sentence appropriately. Example: A triangle has three sides and a square has five sides. A triangle does have three sides, but a square doesn't have five sides, so you would mark that sentence TF.

1. Grapes are a juicy fruit and so are carrots. ___ ___
2. A hen cannot lay an egg but a horse can. ___ ___
3. A dog cannot fly but a bee can. ___ ___
4. My mother is taller than I am, but my baby sister isn't taller than I. ___ ___
5. A house can hop and so can a frog. ___ ___
6. A plant grows but a rock cannot grow. ___ ___
7. Pigs like to eat and lie in cool, wet mud. ___ ___
8. A queen is a woman and so is a king. ___ ___
9. A computer is a machine and so is a television set. ___ ___
10. Children are born with tiny wings and so are kittens. ___ ___

Name _____

Bonus: Write three two-part sentences. One sentence should be completely true, one sentence should be completely false and one sentence should be partly true and partly false.

Name _____

Recipes for What?

Read the directions for making three different desserts found below. Guess what dessert the recipe is for. Write your answer on the line that follows each group of directions.

A.
1. Cream butter with sugar, brown sugar, eggs, vanilla.
2. Mix flour with salt and baking soda. Gradually add to creamed mixture.
3. Stir in chocolate chips and nuts.
4. Drop by tablespoon onto ungreased baking sheet.
5. Bake at 375 degrees for ten minutes or until golden brown.

_____

B.
1. Using the directions on the box, prepare one large box of instant vanilla pudding.
2. Peel and slice three large bananas into bite-sized pieces. Add bananas to pudding.
3. Pour pudding and bananas into a cooled baked pastry shell.
4. Top with whipped cream.

_____

C.
1. Cream butter and sugar until light. Add egg and molasses. Beat thoroughly.
2. Sift together flour, baking soda, ground ginger and cinnamon.
3. Add dry ingredients to creamed mixture alternately with water, beating after each addition.
4. Bake in greased and lightly floured 8 x 8 x 2-inch baking pan at 350 degrees for 35 to 40 minutes or until done. Serve warm, topped with whipped cream if desire.

_____

Bonus: Write the directions for making your favorite dessert. See if a friend can tell you what dessert the directions are for.

What's Inside?

Read the ingredients for four foods found below. Can you guess what food each ingredient list is for? Write your answers on the line found below each list of ingredients.

1. whole wheat, wheat bran, select raisins, sugar, natural flavoring, salt and corn syrup
   _____

2. water, potatoes, clams, partially hydrogenated soy and cottonseed oils, dehydrated onions, celery, modified food starch, butter, nonfat dry milk, bleached enriched flour, natural clam flavoring, salt, sodium caseinate, onion powder, lactose, garlic powder, spice and dipotassium phosphate
   _____

3. cooked beans, beef, water, tomatoes, soy flour, spices, salt, modified food starch, garlic powder, caramel coloring and onion powder
   _____

4. peaches, pears, peach juice, grapes, pineapple tidbits, corn syrup, pear juice, cherries artificially colored red, grape juice, sugar, pineapple juice from concentrate and ascorbic acid
   _____

Name _____

Bonus: distilled vinegar and water, mustard seeds, salt, turmeric, spices and natural flavor

Name _____

Draw It!

In the box below, draw an animal using the following directions:

1. **Draw an animal with the body of a lamb.**
2. **Give the animal a giraffe's neck.**
3. **Give the animal a dog's head.**
4. **The ears of your animal should look like rabbit ears.**
5. **The legs of your animal should look like a pig's legs.**
6. **Give your animal a dragon's tail.**
7. **Add deer antlers.**
8. **Add an elephant's trunk.**
9. **You decide how the eyes should look and draw them, too.**

Bonus: Name your animal using letters or parts of words from the animals listed above.

Name _____

What Day Is It?

Using the calendar, answer the questions found below.

1. **What day is it today, if two days ago it was Wednesday?**
   _____

2. **What day is it today, if three days ago it was Saturday?**
   _____

3. **If today is Tuesday, what day will it be three weeks from now?**
   _____

4. **If today is Friday, what day will it be in one day less than a week?**
   _____

5. **If today is Sunday, what day was it the day before yesterday?**
   _____

6. **If today is Monday, what day was it three days ago?**
   _____

Bonus: If Saturday's date was May 22, what was the date of the Monday before?

Merryville Calendar

In Merryville the calendars have only five days each week. The first day of the week is Jollyday. Jollyday is followed by Happyday, Sillyday, Cheeryday and Funday in that order. Use the Merryville days of the week to answer the questions found below.

1. If it is Sillyday, what day was it yesterday? _____
2. If it is Funday, what day will it be in three more days? _____
3. If the day before yesterday was Happyday, what day is it today? _____
4. If the day after tomorrow will be Funday, what day is it today? _____
5. If yesterday was Jollyday, what day will it be tomorrow? _____
6. If today is Happyday, what day will it be in ten days? _____

Name _____

Bonus: If Merryville has a month called Slapstick that always begins on Funday, what day of the week will the tenth of Slapstick be?

Read and Think

1. If a room has four corners and each corner has a cat, and every cat in the room can see three other cats, how many cats altogether are there in the room?

2. Mr. and Mrs. Martin have seven daughters, and each of the daughters has a brother. How many are there in the Martin family? Explain.

3. If a certain clock chimes the number of the hour on the hour and once every half hour, how many times does the clock chime altogether in one day? Explain.

4. If a man and his sister see a small girl and the man says, "That is my niece," and the woman says, "Well, she isn't my niece," who is the small girl? Explain.

Bonus: Two mothers and two daughters have lunch, but there is only a total of three women at the table. How can that be? Explain.

Name _____

Lamb's Birthday Party

Lamb is planning her own birthday party. She must keep in mind some important facts about her friends' eating habits. Read the facts found below and then help Lamb decide what she will serve to her guests.

Facts:

a. Duck is a vegetarian and loves anything chocolate.
b. Bear likes burgers, shakes and fries a lot, but he will not eat foods that are red or pink.
c. Rabbit will eat anything except foods that begin with the letter C.

1. **Should Lamb plan to serve hamburgers since they are Bear's favorite?** ___
2. **Should Lamb serve a birthday cake or pie?** ___
3. **If Lamb decides to serve a pie, would peach or strawberry pie be best?**
   ___
4. **If Lamb serves ice cream, what would be the best flavor: chocolate, strawberry or vanilla?** ___
5. **Will all of her guests enjoy peanut butter and honey sandwiches?** ___
   ___
6. **Should Lamb serve Coke, strawberry soda or milk to her guests?**
   ___

Name ___

Bonus: Make a grocery list for Lamb's birthday party.

Name _____

Is, Is Not, Is, Is Not!

Fill in the two blanks in each sentence found below with appropriate words. There are many correct answers for this exercise. For example: The blanks in the first sentence could be filled in with *old* and *new* or *expensive* and *inexpensive*.

1. **An antique is** _____ **but not** _____.

2. **A comedian is** _____ **but not** _____.

3. **Liquid is** _____ **but not** _____.

4. **A vacant lot is** _____ **but not** _____.

5. **Fire is** _____ **but not** _____.

6. **A boy is** _____ **but not** _____.

7. **An ant is** _____ **but not** _____.

8. **Lemons are** _____ **but not** _____.

9. **Grass is** _____ **but not** _____.

10. **Popcorn is** _____ **but not** _____.

Bonus: List five words that describe you and five words that do not describe you.

You	Not You
1. _____	1. _____
2. _____	2. _____
3. _____	3. _____
4. _____	4. _____
5. _____	5. _____

Name _____

Four Facts

Assuming that the four statements found below are absolutely true, answer the questions that follow.

Facts:

a. When it snows, Lamb goes to bed one hour early because she has to get up one hour early.

b. Lamb cannot ride her bike to school if it is snowing.

c. It takes Lamb one extra hour to walk to school in the snow.

d. When Lamb rides her bike to school, it takes twenty minutes to get there.

1. It is not snowing. Will Lamb go to bed early? _____

2. If it is not snowing, will it take Lamb twenty minutes to get to school? _____

3. If it is snowing, how long will it take Lamb to walk to school? _____

4. If Lamb is riding her bike to school tomorrow, is it snowing? _____

5. Lamb walked to school yesterday. Did she wear a coat? _____

Bonus: Write a question about Lamb using the four facts found above.

Name _____

Multiple Meanings

Many words have multiple meanings, so the exact meaning must be determined by surrounding words. Draw a line to match each sentence with the appropriate definition for the italicized words in each box.

1. We saw a *bark* whiz by.   tree covering
   The *bark* fell off.   dog's cry
   His *bark* was sharp and loud.   small sailing boat

2. Helen wore her prettiest *dress*.   girl's garment
   The doctor *dressed* the boy's arm.   put on clothes
   Mother said to *dress* quickly.   bandage a wound

3. There was a *mix* of people present.   to confuse
   Don't *mix* me up when I'm counting.   combination
   Use the electric mixer to *mix* the cake. to combine

Bonus: Choose a word with three different meanings. List each meaning and write a sentence to demonstrate each one.

Colorful Details

Use colored pencils or crayons to color code each word in the sentences found below.

Underline who RED.
Underline what BLUE.
Underline when PURPLE.
Underline where GREEN.
Underline how YELLOW.
Underline why ORANGE.

1. Just for fun, Eric happily plays baseball in the park, early Saturday mornings.

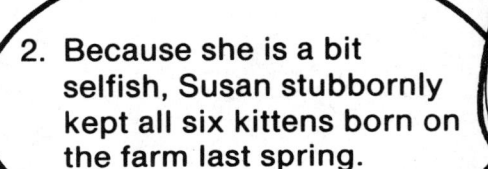

2. Because she is a bit selfish, Susan stubbornly kept all six kittens born on the farm last spring.

3. Rene quickly ran the mile around the field today so she could leave gym class early.

4. Yesterday, Mr. Mac jokingly gave the boys green grapes to eat, in the basement, so he could watch their faces.

5. Every morning at six, Mother gladly runs around the track three times to get her exercise.

6. Sarah usually walks slowly to bed each night because she wants to stay up as late as she can.

Name _____

Bonus: Write a sentence that tells who, what, when, where, how and why.

Copyright © 1990, Good Apple, Inc.

GA1171

Happily Ever After?

The riddles found below can each be answered with the name of a fairy-tale character. The riddles contain clues to the answers.

1. This little boy finally grew up and got a job selling cooking utensils.
   _____

2. This famous emperor gave up his crown and went to live in a nudist colony.
   _____

3. This little boy went back to school and graduated with honors. Later he got a job making marionettes.
   _____

4. When this girl finally came down from her ivory tower, she went to beauty college.
   _____

5. When this little girl realized that she was older than she remembered, she found a job in an applesauce factory.
   _____

Name _____

Bonus: Write your own fairy tale riddle.

Walking Downtown

Use the map found below to answer each question.

1. If Lamb walks three yards east and then two yards south, where will she be?
   _____

2. If Duck waddles three yards south, where will he be?
   _____

3. If Rabbit hops six yards west and then one yard south, where will he be?
   _____

4. If Bear walks four yards north and then six yards east, where will he be?
   _____

5. If Rabbit hops three yards north, where will he be?
   _____

6. If Lamb walks three yards south and then three yards west, where will she be?
   _____

Name _____

Bonus: If Rabbit hops four yards north, five yards west, three yards south, five yards east and then one yard south, where will she be?

Name _____

Which Way?

Imagine that you are standing on the circle, facing north (the direction of the arrow). Use the map to answer the questions found below.

1. If you walk straight ahead, what will you find? _____
2. If you turn to your right and then walk east, what will you find? _____
3. If you want to get to the ocean, what will you have to do? _____
4. What direction is opposite of east? _____
5. What direction is opposite of north? _____
6. If you want to buy a new coat, which direction should you go? _____

Bonus: If you were in the city and wanted to get to the mountains, what direction would you travel?

Name _____

Rhyme Time

1. Name a color that rhymes with BED. _____
2. Name a food that rhymes with HORN. _____
3. Name a flower that rhymes with HOSE. _____
4. Name a number that rhymes with ME. _____
5. Write a girl's name that rhymes with LARRY. _____
6. Write a boy's name that rhymes with JILL. _____
7. Name a shape that rhymes with WEAR. _____
8. Name another animal that rhymes with DOG. _____

Bonus: Name four animals that all rhyme. _____

Name _____

Alike and Different

List one way each word pair is alike and one way each is different. Example: apple/banana—Both are fruits. An apple is red; a banana is not red.

1. **wood/gasoline**
   _____
   _____

2. **balloon/candle**
   _____
   _____

3. **goose/gold**
   _____
   _____

4. **paper/coconut**
   _____
   _____

5. **watermelon/sunflower**
   _____
   _____

6. **ice/vanilla**
   _____
   _____

Bonus: Write a word pair. List three similarities and three differences for the word pair you have chosen.

Word Meaning Zoo

Many animal words have a second meaning. Example: Jay—the bird, J—the tenth letter of the alphabet. Each riddle below can be answered with an animal. The clue for the name of the animal answer is the second meaning for the animal word found in the sentence. For example: This animal is strong enough to carry large loads from one place to another. The answer is *bear*. The words that are the second meaning for the word *bear*, "carry large loads from one place to another," is found in the sentence. After you answer each riddle, underline the second meaning for the animal that is found in the sentence.

1. **This animal hates the sport which uses a line and pole.**
   _____

2. **The baby deer showed pleasure by wagging its tail and licking our hands.**
   _____

3. **This animal is grouchy all the time.**
   _____

4. **This insect moves through the air by moving wings as a bird.**
   _____

5. **The large monkey imitated and mimicked our every action.**
   _____

6. **This farm animal felt meek and afraid.**
   _____

Name _____

Bonus: Write your own double word meaning animal riddle.

Double Meaning Riddles

To solve each riddle found below, you must decide what word fits both clues found in the riddle.

1. This sound can be worn on the finger. _____
2. This tale can be used to knit a sweater. _____
3. This animal can be used to close an envelope. _____
4. This animal can be used to annoy your sister. _____
5. This animal can carry very heavy things. _____
6. This place of enjoyment also means "pale, sunny, average or right."
_____

Name _____

Bonus: Think of a word that has a double meaning and write a riddle for it.

Name _____

Word Associations

Look at the first pair of words in each row and decide how they relate to each other. Then add another word that relates to the third word in the same way. The first one has been completed for you.

1. **win:won   go:went**

2. **man:men   foot:** _____

3. **pencil:lead   pen:** _____

4. **triangle:three   square:** _____

5. **dog:farm   lion:** _____

6. **cage:bars   house:** _____

7. **apple:fruit   carrot:** _____

8. **raisin:grape   prune:** _____

Bonus: Write three sets of word pairs that relate to each other in the same way.

Name _____

You Pick a Pair

Look at the first pair of words in each row and decide how they relate to each other. Then add another pair of words that relate in the same way. The first one has been completed for you.

1. tall:short   night:day

2. happy:glad _____ : _____

3. bird:wing _____ : _____

4. fire:ice _____ : _____

5. hand:glove _____ : _____

6. ship:water _____ : _____

7. roof:house _____ : _____

8. few:many _____ : _____

9. son:daughter _____ : _____

10. two:pair _____ : _____

Bonus: List six pairs of words that all have the same relationship.

Funny Relations

Words can relate to each other in many ways. Use the relationships listed below to describe how the word pairs relate to each other. Write each answer on the blank that follows each pair. Example: glove:hand—relationship is *purpose*.

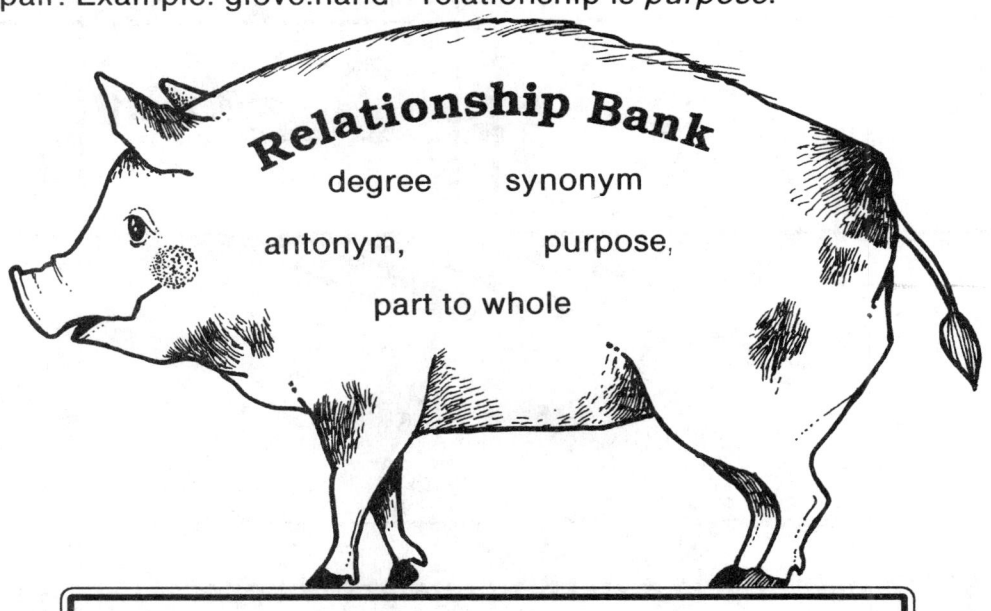

Relationship Bank

degree   synonym

antonym,   purpose,

part to whole

1. shoe:foot _____

2. pink:red _____

3. hat:head _____

4. high:low _____

5. little:tiny _____

6. ring:finger _____

7. finger:hand _____

8. first:primary _____

9. boy:girl _____

Name _____

Bonus: List word pairs to demonstrate each relationship—degree, antonym, synonym, purpose, part to whole.

Reading Pictures

Use the letters of the four pictures found below to answer each question.

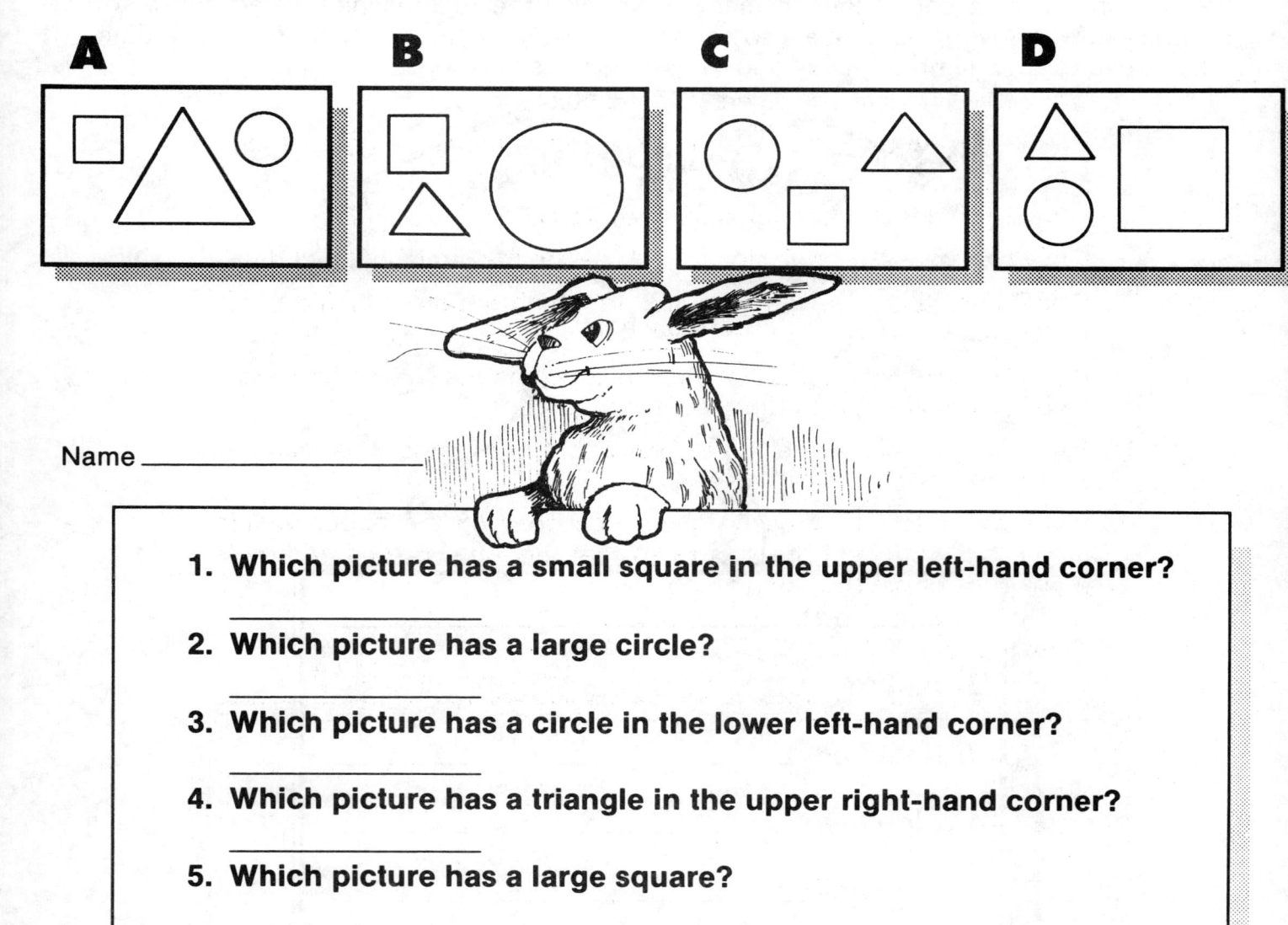

A — square, triangle, circle
B — square, triangle, large circle
C — circle, triangle, square (circle upper-left, triangle upper-right, square lower-middle)
D — triangle, large square, circle

Name _____

1. Which picture has a small square in the upper left-hand corner?
   _____
2. Which picture has a large circle?
   _____
3. Which picture has a circle in the lower left-hand corner?
   _____
4. Which picture has a triangle in the upper right-hand corner?
   _____
5. Which picture has a large square?
   _____
6. Which picture has a triangle in the lower left-hand corner?
   _____
7. Which picture does not have a small triangle in one corner?
   _____
8. Which picture has a small triangle under a small square?
   _____
9. Which picture has three small shapes?
   _____
10. Which picture has a small triangle above a small circle?
    _____

Bonus: Write the step-by-step directions for drawing one of the four pictures found above. See if a friend can figure out which picture you have described.

A Big Surprise

Follow the directions carefully.

1. Draw a large circle in the center of the box.
2. Center two tiny triangles touching the top of the circle about 1 inch apart.
3. Draw a smaller circle inside the large circle.
4. Draw two smaller circles side by side inside the circle you just drew.
5. Place a small square with one side touching the sides of the circle halfway down. Repeat on the other side.
6. Place two small squares with one side touching the sides of the circle at the bottom of the circle about ¼ inch apart.
7. Put two tiny dots inside the largest circle right under the triangles you drew.
8. Place the letter *W* on each square you drew on the opposite side as the side touching the square so that the letter begins and ends on corners of the square.

Name _____

Bonus: Write directions for drawing an animal. Let a friend follow your directions and see how it turns out!

Name _____

Homonym Zoo

Use the homonyms listed in the word bank to complete the sentences found below.

Word Bank

ate, eight   red, read
blue, blew   see, sea
knew, new   two, too
plane, plain   won, one

1. Mother _____ I wore my _____ dress.

2. Our teacher _____ us "The _____ House Mystery."

3. The Bobcats only _____ _____ game.

4. Mark _____ _____ pancakes at breakfast.

5. Sarah _____ up three _____ balloons.

6. He built a _____ from _____ wooden blocks.

7. Max! Eating _____ doughnuts is _____ many.

8. If you look out the window you can _____ the _____.

Bonus: Write three sentences containing homonym pairs.

Lamb's Little House

Lamb lived in a house with her mother, father, six younger brothers and five older sisters. The house was crowded with little lambs playing tag, fighting and making a lot of noise. The bathtub was always being used by one of her sisters. Sometimes the noise didn't bother Lamb, but today she wanted to be alone. She wanted a quiet spot where she could listen to her thoughts. She wanted a place where she could hear herself think. She felt frustrated and angry.

1. **Where did Lamb's brothers play?**
   _____

2. **All together, how many lambs lived in Lamb's house?**
   _____

3. **List three words that might describe Lamb's house.**
   _____   _____   _____

4. **Why was Lamb's house noisy?**
   _____
   _____

5. **Why did Lamb feel angry and frustrated?**
   _____
   _____

6. **What could Lamb do to make herself feel less angry and frustrated?**
   _____
   _____

Bonus: What does it mean to "hear yourself think"?

Name _____

Eight-Letter Words

To solve these puzzles, you must discover the correct eight-letter words. You will have to decide where each word begins, fill in the missing letter and write the word on the blank by each puzzle. Use the clues to help you solve each one.

1. a large four-legged animal

n	t	e
a	■	l
h	e	

_____

2. a summertime beverage

e	m	o
l	■	n
e	d	

_____

3. an animal that kills rats and snakes

	n	g
m	■	o
e	s	o

_____

4. a fast-growing fungus

m	m	u
o	■	s
o		h

_____

5. solid figures with sloping sides

i	d	s
	■	p
a	r	y

_____

6. small spots on the skin often brought out by the sun

r		c
f	■	k
s	e	l

_____

7. covering for cream pies

m	e	
e	■	i
u	g	n

_____

8. a strong animal found in Africa

r	i	
o	■	l
g	s	a

_____

Bonus: Create your own eight-letter puzzle with a clue.

Hinky Pinkies

Hinky pinkies are riddles that require a two-word rhyming answer. Example: A scarlet place to sleep is a *red bed*.

1. A pale red liquid used for writing is _____ _____.
2. A trap for catching household animals is a _____ _____.
3. A drab colored jester is a _____ _____.
4. A group that dines at noon is a _____ _____.
5. An angry employer is a _____ _____.
6. A ten-cent citrus fruit is called a _____ _____.
7. A boat that is really "with it" is a _____ _____.
8. Bird's home that is better than all the other birds' homes is called _____ _____.

Name _____

Bonus: Write clues for three hinky pinkies of your own.

Making Judgements

Read the short paragraph found below. Then answer each question. There are many acceptable answers.

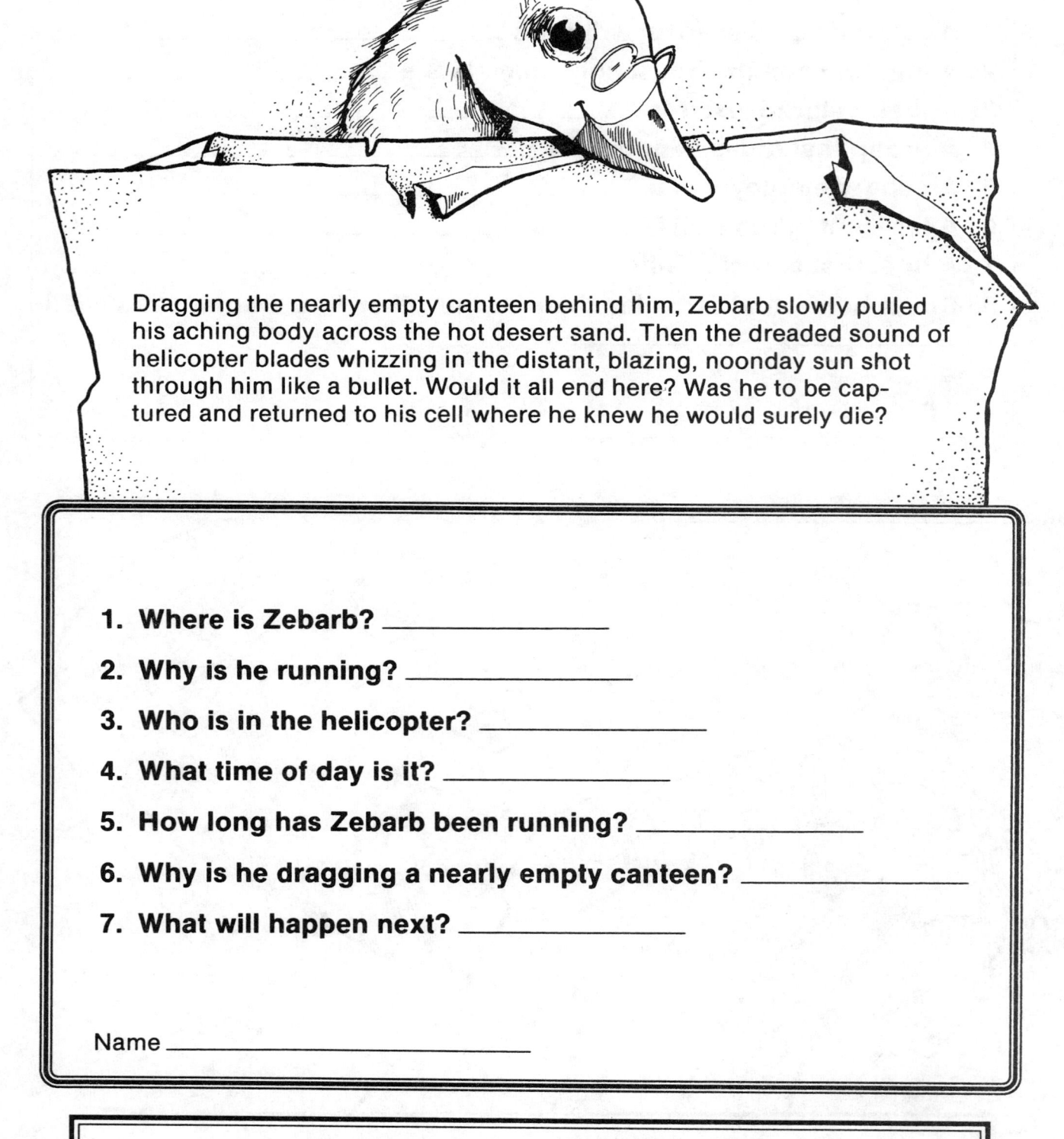

Dragging the nearly empty canteen behind him, Zebarb slowly pulled his aching body across the hot desert sand. Then the dreaded sound of helicopter blades whizzing in the distant, blazing, noonday sun shot through him like a bullet. Would it all end here? Was he to be captured and returned to his cell where he knew he would surely die?

1. Where is Zebarb? _____
2. Why is he running? _____
3. Who is in the helicopter? _____
4. What time of day is it? _____
5. How long has Zebarb been running? _____
6. Why is he dragging a nearly empty canteen? _____
7. What will happen next? _____

Name _____

Bonus: Write the ending to this story.

Generalizations

A generalization means to form a general rule or idea from particular facts or cases without details. Often generalizations are inaccurate. Read the generalization found below. Agree or disagree with it and then answer the questions that follow. Are you of the same opinion after answering the questions?

All boys like to play baseball.   Agree or disagree?

1. Do *all* boys like baseball? _____
2. Do only boys like baseball? _____
3. Do baby boys like to play baseball? _____
4. Do boys in all countries play baseball? _____

Read the generalization found below. Then write four questions to prove that the statement is a generalization.

All girls like to wear pretty dresses.

1. _____
2. _____
3. _____
4. _____

Name _____

Bonus: Write a generalization that you feel is absolutely true.

Name _____

Reading Up and Down

To discover the secret message, begin with the first vertical row and read the letters from top to bottom, recording each letter found to the left of the dots. Then record each letter found to the left of the dots in the second vertical row, etc.

Secret Message: ___ ___ ___ ___ ___ ___ ___, ___

A						•		•								•	•					•				
B				•																						
C										•								•		•	•					
D					•				•																	
E		•										•	•				•		•			•				
F	•										•															
G																										
H											•				•				•							
I		•																			•				•	
J																										
K							•																			
L													•													
M																								•		
N			•						•																•	•
O						•	•													•		•			•	
P																							•			
Q																										
R	•												•						•	•						
S				•			•																			•
T															•											
U														•												
V																										
W																										
X																										
Y																										
Z																										

Copyright © 1990, Good Apple, Inc.

GA1171

Name _____

Reading Matchup

To discover the secret word, draw lines connecting the words (on the left) with the appropriate definition (on the right). Then write the letters that are bisected by lines, from top to bottom, in the appropriate blanks.

Secret Word: __ __ __ __ __ __ __ __

1. slice •
2. strike •
3. gadget •
4. protest •
5. purple •
6. sea •
7. sling •
8. green •
9. potato •
10. separate •
11. trap •

f
v
r   i
 e
n   d
         o
    e   s
 h   l
         i
          p

• hitting something
• thin piece cut from something else
• body of salt water
• speak out against
• ancient weapon
• color that is a mixture of blue and red
• plant used as a vegetable
• small mechanical thing
• device for catching things
• divided into groups
• not ripe

Bonus: Unscramble the rest of the letters to spell another word.

Name _____

True or False?

To discover the secret message, read each statement found below and decide if it is true or false. If a statement is true, write the first letter of that statement in the square on the left of the sentence. If the statement is false, write the first letter of that statement in the square to the right of the sentence. Transfer the letters reading down the left column and then down the right column in the appropriate blanks.

Secret Message: __ __ __ __ __ __ __ __ __ __ __ __ __
__ __ __ __ __ __ __ __ __ __ __ __ .

TRUE　　　　　　　　　　　　　　　　　　　　　　**FALSE**

☐ 1. *Flick* means a light, quick stroke. ☐
☐ 2. Rats eat cheese. ☐
☐ 3. Tomatoes grow underground. ☐
☐ 4. Onions grow on tall trees. ☐
☐ 5. Islands are surrounded by water. ☐
☐ 6. Elephants have tusks. ☐
☐ 7. Bees make jelly. ☐
☐ 8. Nests are homes for birds. ☐
☐ 9. Dogs come in many sizes. ☐
☐ 10. Spearmint is a plant. ☐
☐ 11. Eggplant is orange and blue. ☐
☐ 12. Hippopotamus is an animal. ☐
☐ 13. *Swift* means very slowly. ☐
☐ 14. *I* is a vowel. ☐
☐ 15. Hound is a breed of cat. ☐
☐ 16. Pear is a soft, yellow fruit. ☐
☐ 17. Abraham Lincoln is president. ☐
☐ 18. Nutcrackers are used to crack nuts. ☐
☐ 19. Egypt is a country. ☐
☐ 20. Eighteen comes after seventeen. ☐
☐ 21. Rodents are fish and birds. ☐
☐ 22. Decals are transferable. ☐
☐ 23. Summer is one of four seasons. ☐
☐ 24. Eyes are used to hear sounds. ☐
☐ 25. *Decade* means one hundred years. ☐

Copyright © 1990, Good Apple, Inc.　　　　　　GA1171

Crossword Puzzle

Across
1. a round, crispy dessert
4. opposite of even
5. something to eat with bacon
8. grown-up puppies are called

Down
1. fluffy and white, floats in the sky
2. something unusual and different
3. frozen water
6. opposite of come
7. opposite of isn't

Name _____

Name _____

Rhyming Animals

If you replace each animal found in the sentences below with a rhyming animal, the sentences will make sense.

1. I am worried that my dog has bees.
   _____

2. My bat ran up a tree and cannot get down.
   _____

3. Quails are the largest creatures on earth.
   _____

4. My dog can hop from lily pad to lily pad.
   _____

5. I had a lady slug but it flew away.
   _____

6. One hundred years ago, many crows roamed free.
   _____

Bonus: List a pair of rhyming animals that are not used above.

Scrambled Anagrams

Anagrams are two words spelled with the same letters. Example: ate, tea. Answer each riddle below by unscrambling a word to spell a new word.

1. **Unscramble HOES and you will have something to wear on your foot.** _____

2. **Unscramble POTS and you'll have a good name for a dog.**
   _____

3. **Unscramble RATS and you'll have something that twinkles.**
   _____

4. **Unscramble ARM and you will get an animal.**
   _____

5. **Unscramble NET to get a number.**
   _____

6. **Unscramble BEARD to get something good to eat.**
   _____

7. **Unscramble SCAT to get something for a broken arm.**
   _____

8. **Unscramble TABLES to get a place to keep horses.**
   _____

Bonus: Unscramble the word *vile* to spell three other words.

Name _____

Anagrams

An anagram is a word spelled by rearranging the letters of another word. Example: stop and pots. Carefully read the sentences found below. Then find and underline the two anagrams in each sentence.

1. Eric couldn't quite eat all of his brown rice and vegetables.

2. We had great fun picking lemons and melons when we went to my grandfather's farm.

3. When mother cleaned, she rearranged things. She put the lamp next to the chair and the sofa near the palm.

4. While Dad barbecued the steaks, my sister Susan and I put on our skates and got some exercise.

5. The fruit was cheap, so I bought apples, bananas, cherries and a peach.

6. The beat of the astronaut's heart increased as he left planet Earth headed for the moon.

Bonus: Write a sentence with a pair of anagrams in it.

Name _____

Five Fantastic Gifts!

When Duck turned five, his father gave him five fantastic gifts. On each package was a riddle. Read the riddles on Duck's packages and decide what is inside each present.

1. When it's dark
   We'll both be bright.
   If you fill me with C's,
   Then we both can see.

2. Look in me
   And you will see
   Details of things
   Smaller than a flea.

3. With my mirrors
   And contoured glass,
   You can see the moon,
   Stars and past.

4. I don't need
   A house you see.
   I carry mine on
   The back of me.

5. Look deep inside
   Just shake and wind,
   And colorful designs
   You will find.

_____   _____

_____   _____

_____

Bonus: Write a riddle for the present you would most like to receive on your next birthday.

Name _____

Hidden Colors

Carefully read the sentences found below. Then look for a color word hidden in each sentence. The letters of the word can be found in parts of two words that are together.

Example: She brough(t an) apple to the teacher. Underline each color word.

1. Bob lacks character, but he doesn't lack self-confidence.
2. Mother said to cover Ed, my puppy, with a blanket.
3. On Halloween, I will dress as a ghost or angel.
4. Pass me my other spur, please, so I can get ready to go riding.
5. I seem to be growing older every day.
6. She received a flowerpot and a plant for her birthday.
7. Don't yell! Owls are common in this area.
8. The Girl Scout leader will pin Kathy and Sharon at the next meeting.

Bonus: Write a sentence with a hidden color word in it.

Name _____

Who Brought What?

Carefully read the story found below and then answer each question.

> At Stuart School pet show, seven children—Barbara, Joshua, Jerry, Amber, Mark, Kim, and Danny—brought pets. The animals brought included one of the following: fish, bird, hamster, snake, cat, dog and rabbit. Barbara's cat was chased by Joshua's pet. Jerry brought his pet in a bowl. Danny's hamster cage was heavier than Mark's bird cage. Amber didn't bring the snake; she's afraid of snakes.

1. Who brought the dog? _____
2. Who brought the hamster? _____
3. Who carried the heaviest cage? _____
4. What did Kim bring? _____
5. Who owns the fish? _____
6. Who brought the rabbit? _____

Bonus: Make a list of the seven children and write the appropriate animal next to each child's name.

Name _____

Relationships

Read the short story found below and then answer the six questions that follow.

> Susan, a teenager, is baby-sitting the twins, Ted and Tom. Susan knows all about the twins because Tom is her brother Jack's best friend, and Ted is her youngest brother Jerry's best friend.

1. Name the oldest child in the story.
   _____

2. What are the names of the twins?
   _____

3. Is Jerry Tom's best friend?
   _____

4. Is Jerry or Jack the oldest?
   _____

5. What are Susan's brothers' names?
   _____

6. What is the name of the twin's baby-sitter?
   _____

Bonus: If one boy mentioned in the story is younger than all the other children in the story, what is his name?

Name _____

Favorite Colors

Carefully read the story found below; then answer the eight questions that follow.

> Sarah Brown's favorite color is pink. Ruth Silver's favorite color is purple. Roberta White's favorite color is yellow. Laura Black's favorite color is green.

1. **Whose favorite color is green?**
   _____

2. **Whose favorite color is pink?**
   _____

3. **What is the last name of the girl whose favorite color is green?**
   _____

4. **What is the last name of the girl whose favorite color is purple?**
   _____

5. **Is Laura's last name Black or Green?**
   _____

6. **What is Roberta's favorite color?**
   _____

7. **What is the last name of the girl whose favorite color is pink?**
   _____

8. **What is the last name of the girl whose favorite color is yellow?**
   _____

Bonus: Make a list of ten friends and their favorite colors.

Name _____

Occupations

Carefully read the story found below; then answer the eight questions that follow.

> Andrew's father is a barber and his mother is a waitress. Max's father is an artist; his mother is a teacher. Charlie's father is a judge; his mother is an actress. William's father is a cook; his mother is a dentist.

1. **Whose father needs scissors to do his job?**
   _____

2. **Whose father works with food?**
   _____

3. **Whose mother works with food?**
   _____

4. **Whose mother might wear rubber gloves when she works?**
   _____

5. **Whose mother goes to school to work?**
   _____

6. **Whose father is asked to make very important decisions?**
   _____

7. **Whose mother might say, "Open wide," when she is working?**
   _____

8. **What is the actress' son's name?**
   _____

Bonus: Whose father might do his work at home?

Name _____

What Day of the Week?

Use the calendar for July found below to answer each question.

M	T	W	T	F	S	S

JULY

1. If the first day of the month falls on Thursday, what day of the week will be the Fourth of July? _____

2. If the first day of the month falls on Monday, what day of the week will it be on July 10? _____

3. If the first day of the month falls on Friday, what day of the week will it be on July 13? _____

4. If the Fourth of July is celebrated on a Monday, what day of the week was July 1? _____

5. If July 11 is on a Saturday, what day of the week will it be on July 18? _____

Bonus: If the first day of July is on Monday, what day of the week will it be on the last day of July?

Name _____

Bez, Poks and Deeks

Carefully read the story found below; then answer each question.

> On the planet Zip, the people eat fruit a lot like that which is grown on Earth, except the flavors and colors are different. A BEZ looks like a red banana and tastes like sour grapes. A POK looks like a blue apple and tastes like a banana. DEEKS look like orange-colored grapes and are watermelon-flavored.

1. Does a BEZ taste sweet or sour? _____
2. Which fruit tastes like a banana? _____
3. Which fruit grows in bunches? _____
4. What color is a POK? _____
5. What color is the watermelon-flavored fruit? _____
6. Is the blue fruit of Zip sweet or sour? _____

Bonus: Make up another fruit grown on planet Zip. Describe its color and flavor.

Name _____

Snack Time

Carefully read the story found below; then answer each question.

> Anna and Peter love popcorn; it is their favorite snack. Rose likes popcorn; but it isn't her favorite. Peter and Rose both dislike peanuts and neither one ever eats them. Rose's favorite snack is pretzels; she just loves them. Anna dislikes pretzels and never eats them. Anna likes peanuts, but they aren't her favorite. Peter likes pretzels, but he doesn't have them very often.

1. Who loves pretzels? _____
2. Who dislikes pretzels? _____
3. How does Anna feel about peanuts? _____
4. Which children dislike peanuts? _____
5. What seems to be the most popular snack? _____
6. If Anna is having Peter as a guest, should she serve him popcorn or peanuts? _____
7. If Peter wants to give away a bag of pretzels, should he offer them to Anna or Rose? _____
8. Which snack is loved by one child, liked by one child and disliked by one child? _____

Bonus: How would you rate popcorn, peanuts and pretzels?

Name _____

Going to School

Carefully read the clues found below; then answer each question.

   a. Five children, Don, Judy, Heather, Casey and Danny live on the same street.
   b. Two of the children ride the bus to school.
   c. As many walk as ride the bus.
   d. Don always goes alone.

1. Judy doesn't walk to school. How does she get there? _____

2. Heather always goes to school with Danny. How do they get to school? _____

3. Who rides his bike to school? _____

4. How does Casey get to school? _____

5. Who gets to school the same way Judy does? _____

Bonus: How many children walk to school? How many ride to school?

Name _____

The Great Race!

Carefully read the clues found below; then answer each question.

a. Four boys—Lee, Casey, Eric and Luke—ran a race.
b. Eric didn't come in third.
c. Luke came in first or last.
d. Casey ran faster than Lee.
e. Lee came in first or last.

1. Did Luke come in first or last?

2. Did Eric run faster than Casey? _____

3. Who came in last? _____

4. Was Lee faster than Casey? _____

5. Which two boys ran slower than Eric? _____

6. Who came in third? _____

7. Who came in right after Eric? _____

8. How many boys ran faster than Lee? _____

Bonus: List the steps you used to figure out which boy came in first, second, third and fourth.

Answer Key

Wacky Words page 1
1. highlight
2. She is overjoyed.
3. ladies before gentlemen
4. eggs over easy
5. What goes up, must come down.
6. I'm just beside myself.
7. Little League
8. pizza with everything on it

Picture That! page 2
1. 1,4
2. 1
3. 2,3
4. 2,4
5. 1
6. 1
7. 2
8. 4

The Birthday Party page 3
1. eight
2. three
3. two
4. one
5. one
6. one, two
Bonus: horse, fish, octopus, lion, ladybug, snake, bird, chicken, butterfly, dog, sheep, bear

Happyville Citizens page 4
Lamb: pink bow, orange dress, white wool
Rabbit: blue shorts, brown fur
Bear: green pants, green umbrella, black fur
Duck: vest color will vary, orange bill and feet, yellow feathers

What's Wrong Here? page 5
1. The dog has a plant on its head.
2. There is a snake on the chair.
3. The Y card is upside down.
4. The clock has no hands and is numbered wrong.
5. There is a frog by the lunch boxes.
6. The rabbit has an open umbrella.
7. The pig has a pizza on his head.
8. The porcupine is wearing a swimming cap.
9. The porcupine is sitting on a toadstool.
10. The calendar says *July*, but it's snowing outside.
11. There are no numbers on the calendar.
12. There is a clown in the hall.

Reading Pictures, page 6
summer/winter, night/day, three/four, girls/boys, park/school, girl/boy, her/his, he/she, cat/dog, cry/laugh, sad/funny, following/ahead

It's No Picnic, page 7
picnic: sandwich, watermelon, chips, pickles, napkin, cupcakes, apple, fork, soda, paper plate
school: crayons, pencil, math book, homework, lunch money, something to share

Circus Fun page 8
1. 5
2. 2
3. 1
4. 18
5. 3

Draw Your Own Story page 9
Pictures will vary.

You Must Decide page 10
1. 1,2,4
2. 4
3. 2
4. 1
5. 1,4
6. 3

Out the Window! page 11
1. 2
2. 1
3. 3 or 4
4. 1
5. 4
6. 3
7. 1
8. Answer will vary.
Bonus: Answers will vary.

Following Directions page 12
A good companion makes any journey seem shorter.

Simon Sez page 13
small girl: blond, straight hair; red dress; purple flowers in basket; tall girl: red curly hair, orange dress; blue socks; sun in upper right-hand corner, green grass

Coloring the Animals page 14
1. owl: brown
2. cat: orange and white striped
3. rabbit: white with black spots
4. ladybug: red with black spots
5. dog: white with black spots
6. squirrel: gray
7. mouse: black

Happyville House page 15
Lamb's house: red, green roof, purple door, yellow bushes on both sides. Duck's house: purple, orange roof, blue door, red flag on mailbox. Rabbit's house: yellow, red roof, pink door, green tree between Rabbit's and Duck's houses.

Coloring Clowns page 16
Colors will vary.

Changing Letters page 17
Be a friend to yourself and others will also want to.

Hidden Words page 18
Answers may vary.
1. nightmare/mare
2. heart/ear
3. butterfly/fly
4. marmalade/arm
5. cricket/Rick
6. orangutan/tan
Bonus: aristocrat/rat

Conundrums page 19
1. hare (hair)
2. whale
3. crab
4. duck
5. bear
6. caterpillar
7. ant (aunt)
8. bat
Bonus: gnu (new)

Reading a Graph page 20
1. 17
2. chocolate chip
3. 1
4. peanut butter
5. 2
6. Answers will vary.

Check, Please! page 21

	can read	talks	needs water	jumps	makes noise
frog					
boys	✓	✓	✓	✓	✓
plants			✓		
girls	✓	✓	✓	✓	✓
flower			✓		
fish			✓		
tiger			✓	✓	✓
stick					
leaf					
computer					✓

Bonus: me

Riddle Names page 22
1. Bill, Bill Fold (billfold)
2. Tim, Tim Id (timid)
3. Tom, Tom Tom (tom-tom)
4. Ed, Ed U. Kate (educate)
5. Jay, Jay Walk (jaywalk)
Bonus: Vic, Vic Torian (Victorian)

Scrambled Word Riddles page 23
1. pineapple
2. hamburger
3. sweater
4. kitten
Bonus: elephant

True or False? page 24
1. TF
2. FF
3. TT
4. TT
5. FT
6. TT
7. TT
8. TF
9. TT
10. FF

Recipes for What? page 25
1. chocolate chip cookies
2. banana cream pie
3. gingerbread

What's Inside? page 26
1. Raisin Bran
2. clam chowder
3. chili
4. fruit cocktail
Bonus: mustard

Draw It! page 27
Pictures will vary.

What Day Is It? page 28
1. Friday
2. Tuesday
3. Tuesday
4. Thursday
5. Friday
6. Friday
Bonus: May 17

Merryville Calendar page 29
1. Happyday
2. Sillyday
3. Cheeryday
4. Sillyday
5. Sillyday
6. Happyday
Bonus: Cheeryday

Read and Think page 30
1. four cats (Each cat sees the other three cats.)
2. ten people (seven daughters, one son and two parents)
3. one hundred and eighty times 12 for each half hour + 1 + 2 + 3 + 4 + 5 + 6 + 7 + 8 + 9 + 10 + 11 + 12 = number of strikes in 12 hours (90). In one day (24 hours) it will be two times that number (180).
4. The girl is the woman's daughter and the man's niece.
Bonus: One woman is the mother of one woman and the daughter of the other.

Lamb's Birthday Party page 31
1. No. Duck is a vegetarian.
2. Pie. Rabbit won't eat (c)ake.
3. Peach. Bear won't eat strawberries (red).
4. Vanilla. Bear won't eat strawberry (pink) ice cream.
5. Yes
6. Milk. Rabbit won't drink (C)oke. Bear won't drink strawberry soda (pink).
Bonus: peach pie, vanilla ice cream, bread, peanut butter, honey and milk

Is, Is Not, Is, Is Not! page 32
Answers will vary.
1. old, new
2. funny, sad
3. wet, dry
4. empty, full
5. hot, cold
6. young, old (short, tall), etc.
7. little, big (animal, plant), etc.
8. sour, sweet
9. green, blue
10. white, black

Four Facts page 33
1. no
2. yes
3. one extra hour
4. no
5. yes, probably
Bonus: Answers will vary.

Multiple Meanings page 34
1. We saw bark whiz by. (small sailing boat) The bark fell off. (tree covering) His bark was sharp and loud. (dog's cry)
2. Helen wore her prettiest dress. (girl's garment) The doctor dressed the boy's arm. (bandage a wound) Mother said to dress quickly. (put on clothes)
3. There was a mix of people present. (combination) Don't mix me up when I'm counting. (to confuse) Use the electric mixer to mix the cake. (to combine)

Colorful Details page 35
1. who: Eric, what: plays, when: early Saturday mornings, where: in the park, how: happily, why: just for fun
2. who: Susan, what: kept, when: last spring, where: on the farm how: stubbornly, why: because she is a bit selfish
3. who: Rene, what: ran, when: today, where: around the field, how: quickly, why: so she could leave gym class early
4. who: Mr. Mac, what: gave, when: yesterday, where: in the basement, how: jokingly, why: so he could watch their faces
5. who: Mother, what: runs, when: every morning at six, where: around the track, how: gladly, why: to get her exercise
6. who: Sarah, what: walks, when: each night, where: to bed, how: slowly, why: because she wants to stay up as late as she can

Happily Ever After? page 36
1. Peter Pan
2. Emperor of "The Emperor's New Clothes"
3. Pinocchio
4. Rapunzel
5. Sleeping Beauty

Walking Downtown page 37
1. Rabbit's house
2. Rabbit's house
3. Bear's house
4. Duck's house
5. Duck's house
6. Bear's house
Bonus: Home again!

Which Way? page 38
1. mountains
2. city
3. Turn around and walk south
Bonus: northwest
4. west
5. south
6. east

Rhyme Time page 39
1. red
2. corn
3. rose
4. three
5. Mary
6. Bill
7. square
8. hog
Bonus: cat, rat, gnat, bat

Alike and Different page 40
Answers will vary.
1. Both will burn. Wood is not man-made; gasoline is man-made.
2. Both need air. Candles are lit with a match; balloons are not lit with a match.
3. Both begin with the letter G. A goose is alive; gold is not alive.
4. Both are usually white. You can eat coconut; you cannot eat paper.
5. Both can grow in a garden. Watermelon grows on the ground; sunflowers do not grow on the ground.
6. Both are used to make ice cream. Ice is kept frozen; vanilla is not kept frozen.

Word Meaning Zoo page 41
1. fish: sport which uses a line and pole
2. fawn: showed pleasure by wagging its tail and licking our hands
3. crab: grouchy
4. fly: moves through the air by moving wings as a bird
5. ape: imitated and mimicked
6. cow: felt meek and afraid

Double Meaning Riddles page 42
1. ring
2. yarn
3. seal
4. bug
5. bear
6. fair

Word Associations page 43
Answers will vary.
1. go:went
2. foot:feet
3. pen:ink
4. square:four
5. lion:zoo
6. house:walls
7. carrot:vegetable
8. prune:plum

You Pick a Pair page 44
Answers will vary.

Funny Relations page 45
1. purpose
2. degree
3. purpose
4. antonym
5. synonym
6. purpose
7. part to whole
8. synonym
9. antonym

Reading Pictures page 46
1. A
2. B
3. D
4. C
5. D
6. B
7. A
8. B
9. C
10. D

A Big Surprise page 47
Picture may be of a pig.

Homonym Zoo page 48
1. knew, new
2. read, Red
3. won, one
4. ate, eight
5. blew, blue
6. plane, plain
7. two, too
8. see, sea

73

Copyright © 1990, Good Apple, Inc.

GA1171

Lamb's Little House page 49
1. In the house
2. 14
3. Answers will vary. small, crowded, noisy
4. Crowded and small, full of lambs, etc.
5. Lamb needed a quiet place.
6. Go for a quiet walk. (will vary)

Eight-Letter Words page 50
1. elephant
2. lemonade
3. mongoose
4. mushroom
5. pyramids
6. freckles
7. meringue
8. gorillas

Hinky Pinkies page 51
1. pink ink
2. pet net
3. brown clown
4. lunch bunch
5. cross boss
6. dime lime
7. hip ship
8. best nest

Making Judgements page 52
Answers will vary. There are no correct answers.
1. in the desert
2. from the police
3. police
4. noon
5. days
6. Because he is hot, tired and thirsty.
7. Answers will vary.

Generalizations page 53
1. no
2. no
3. no
4. no
Answers will vary.
Examples: 1. Some girls do not like to wear dresses.
2. Not only girls like to wear dresses; women like to wear dresses, too.
3. Do baby girls understand what they are wearing?
4. Do girls like to wear pretty dresses when they play? If it is cold?

Reading Up and Down page 54
Friends, books and a cheerful heart are choice companions.

Reading Matchup page 55
friendship
1. slice, thin piece cut from something else
2. strike, hitting something
3. gadget, small mechanical thing
4. protest, speak out against
5. purple, color that is a mxiture of blue and red
6. sea, body of salt water
7. sling, ancient weapon
8. green, not ripe
9. potato, plant used as a vegetable
10. separate, divided into groups
11. trap, device for catching things
Bonus: love

True or False? page 56
Friendship needs to be shared.

Crossword Puzzle page 57
Across
1. cookie
4. odd
5. egg
8. dog

Down
1. cloud
2. odd
3. ice
6. go
7. is

Rhyming Animals page 58
1. fleas
2. cat or rat
3. whale
4. frog
5. bug
6. buffalo
Bonus: veil, evil, live

Scrambled Anagrams page 59
1. shoe
2. Spot
3. star
4. ram
5. ten
6. bread
7. cast
8. stable

Anagrams page 60
1. Eric, rice
2. lemons, melons
3. lamp, palm
4. steaks, skates
5. cheap, peach
6. heart, earth

Five Fantastic Gifts! page 61
1. flashlight
2. microscope
3. turtle
4. kaleidoscope
5. telescope

Hidden Colors page 62
1. Bo(B lack)s
2. cove(r Ed)
3. (or ange)l
4. s(pur, ple)ase,
5. growi(g old)er
6. po(t an)d
7. (yell ow)ls
8. (pin K)athy

Who Brought What? page 63
1. Joshua
2. Danny
3. Danny
4. snake
5. Jerry
6. Amber
Bonus: Barbara, cat; Joshua, dog; Jerry, fish; Amber, rabbit; Mark, bird; Kim, snake; Danny, hampster

Relationships page 64
1. Susan
2. Ted, Tom
3. no
4. Jack
5. Jerry, Jack
6. Susan
Bonus: Jerry

Favorite Colors page 65
1. Laura Black
2. Sarah Brown
3. Black
4. Silver
5. Black
6. yellow
7. Brown
8. White

Occupations page 66
1. Andrew's (barber) or Max's (artist)
2. William's
3. Andrew's
4. William's
5. Max's
6. Charlie's
7. William's
8. Charlie
Bonus: Max's

What Day of the Week? page 67
1. Sunday
2. Wednesday
3. Wednesday
4. Friday
5. Saturday
Bonus: Saturday

Bez, Poks and Deeks page 68
1. sour
2. pok
3. deeks
4. blue
5. orange
6. sweet

Snack Time page 69
1. Rose
2. Anna
3. likes them
4. Peter, Rose
5. popcorn
6. popcorn
7. Rose
8. pretzels

Going to School page 70
1. rides the bus
2. walk
3. Don
4. rides the bus
5. Casey
Bonus: 2 walk, 3 ride

The Great Race! page 71
1. first
2. yes
3. Lee
4. no
5. Casey, Lee
6. Casey
7. Casey
8. three
Bonus: Statement five says that Lee came in first or last and statement four states that Casey ran faster than Lee, so we know Lee didn't come in first and must have come in last. Statement three says Luke came in first or last and since we now know that Lee came in last, Luke must have come in first. Statement two states that Eric didn't come in third and we know he didn't come in first or fourth, so Eric must have come in second, which leaves Casey in third place.